The Magic of Thailand

CONTENTS

The Allure of Thailand

Thailand, as a whole, is defined by its tropical location right in the heart of southeast Asia, a fact that helps account for the steamy heat, lush green forests, flood plains, patchwork of rice fields and multitude of golden beaches and stunning coral reefs.

The variety of environments, combined with an equally rich culture and the remarkably open and friendly disposition of the people, attracts millions of foreign visitors to a country which, invariably, weaves its magic spell and fosters the wish to return and experience more.

Thailand's length, some 1800km (1118 miles) north to south, helps account for its impressive topography that distinguishes it in terms of landscape, climate and lifestyle. The far south, bordering with Malaysia, lies just over six degrees north of the Equator, while in the far north the border with Laos and Myanmar (Burma) is only a few degrees away from the Tropic of Cancer.

Above A young monk enters the Wat Chedi Luang in Chiang Mai. Destroyed by an earthquake in the 16th century, the Wat is famous for its Jade Buddha which is being restored to its former glory.

Right A little dancer of Chiang Mai, northern Thailand, proudly displays her traditional, handcrafted costume, intricately embroidered and decorated with beads.

GEOGRAPHY

Some 60 million people live in Thailand, which covers an area of around 0.5 million square kilometres. The heart of the country is a mainly rice-producing area and the region is characterized by modestly-sized, family-run farms.

The capital city of Bangkok, on the coast to the south, provides the commercial infrastructure that underpins the country's economy. With around one in six of the nation's population residing in the greater Bangkok area, this metropolis is a human powerhouse of social, economic and political energy.

The north of Thailand has its own geographic identity, a land of mountains and river valleys peopled by hardy hill tribes who, a few generations back, did not even conceive of themselves as Thais. Modern means of communication and transport, plus the advent of mass tourism, have helped to open up the northern region but the people have retained their strong sense of individuality.

The northeast region of Thailand also has its own cultural identity rooted in geography. Mountains to the west and south have isolated it somewhat and the relatively poor land has made it a harsh environment for farmers who struggle to make a living from their paddy fields,

Above The seascape of Phang Nga National Park, with its jungles, mangrove swamps and lunar-like karst formations is home to some of Asia's stranger creatures, such as the water monitor, a dragon-like lizard that can grow to a length of 2.5m (8ft).

forcing many of the children to migrate to Bangkok in search of work and an easier life.

The more tropical southern region of the country supports vast rubber plantations rather than rice paddies, while western Thailand is characterized by mountains and forests – a landscape in the process of being changed by logging companies.

Above It is harvest time in Chiang Rai province and the rice fields have turned a deep orange yellow. This is the busiest time for farmers and the entire family will help to bring in the yield.

Left The ancient forests contain thousands of species of plants and animals, all competing for valuable light and nutrients.

Below One of the many waterfalls at Erawan National Park in Kanchanaburi province, that feed the Khwae Yai river.

Left Thai fishermen launch their flimsy vessels in a strange seascape of jutting limestone pillars and jungle-backed empty beaches.

Below In Chiang Mai, enthusiastic participants of the Songkran festival throw water over each other to greet the arrival of the rainy season.

Right Breathtaking Phi Phi Island has all the ingredients for an unforgettable holiday: unspoilt exotic beaches surrounding aquamarine bays fringed by lush tropical growth.

CLIMATE

Being a tropical country, Thailand is subject to the effect of monsoons on its climate. The result is a set of seasons characterized by dry periods that last from two months in the deep south to six months in the far north, and annual wet spells that can bring rainfall on an average of two days in every three. The tropical heat can soar beyond 40°C (104°F) during the dry season, and with humidity averaging well over 70 per cent, woe betide visitors from colder climes who fail to relax their pace or adequately protect their bodies from the searing rays of the sun.

In parts of the north, on the other hand, the cooler months see temperatures dropping to below 15°C (59°F) and a thin shirt leaves you yearning for a decent sweater or pullover. Needless to say, the variable climate produces an endless topic of conversation for Thais. For rice farmers, especially, the weather is crucial, because the pattern of rainfall determines the agricultural calendar. The importance of the arrival of rain that marks the end of a dry season, so essential for the cultivation of rice, is celebrated with gusto. Many first-time tourists experience this when they find themselves suddenly drenched in buckets of water – the legitimate target of fun during a water-throwing festival. In farming communities, religious ceremonies are scheduled to coincide with the arrival of a wet season.

COASTS, REEFS & DIVING

The western coastline of southern Thailand faces the Andaman Sea and beyond that the Indian Ocean, while the eastern coastline and the Gulf of Thailand look to the South China Sea. The result, a remarkably rich and diverse marine life, accounts for the valuable contribution that fishing makes to Thailand's economy, as well as the vital importance of seafood in Thai cuisine.

Thailand's coral reefs are quite spectacular, especially those in the Andaman Sea which have not as yet suffered from the over-exploitation that has seen the virtual destruction of many reefs in the Gulf of Thailand. The Bangkok region is responsible for most of the large-scale pollution that is endangering marine life. Paradoxically, tourism contributed to the ecological damage as resorts and operators strove to satisfy the demands of visitors who came to dive and appreciate the stunning beaches that adorn many of the smaller islands. Mass tourism to tiny islands results in sewerage and rubbish disposal problems and eco-ignorant divers vandalize reefs by anchoring on them, grounding boats on soft coral, collecting shells and flaying their fins about in delicate ecosystems.

Below The beautiful Ap Ton Sai beach on Phi Phi Island is one of Thailand's most popular destinations. Here you can enjoy beautiful walks, snorkelling, as well as a lively nightlife and luxurious accommodation.

On the positive side, the world-renowned Surin and Similan islands are now national marine parks. The five islands of the Surin Islands National Marine Park, over 50km (31 miles) off the western coast and just south of the border with Myanmar, are home to some of the finest colonies of coral in Thailand. There are nine Similan islands, 80km (50 miles) northwest of Phuket, and divers from all over the world come here to experience the coral life.

Left Fantasea Reef in Mu Koh Similan Marine National Park is covered in soft coral and large gorgonians – incredible splendour awaits divers.

Above Naganoi Pearl Farm on Phuket Island is worth a visit to learn how pearls are produced, harvested, graded and made into jewellery.

Above The aptly named harlequin shrimp (*Hymenocera picta*) is just one of many colourful inhabitants of Thailand's marine reserves.

Above It has been said that *Cocos nucifera*, the coconut palm, has as many uses as there are days in the year. Coconut oil, milk, and flesh provide food while the husk provides coir, used in matting and weaving. The fronds supply material for roofing, while the liquid inside the shell makes palm wine.

Left Thailand's many habitats support numerous species of orchid, and the country's national flower is the dendrobium. Decorating forests and savanna around the countryside, the orchid is also a major export industry, one that earns Thailand millions of dollars annually.

Right Bamboo is a multi-use natural product of Thailand. From furniture to builders' scaffolding planks, cooking utensils and home-made firecrackers, bead curtains, jewellery and fuel for the cooking stove, bamboo in its many forms is an essential part of Thai life.

FLORA

Tropical climate and seasonal variations account for the rich flora of Thailand: from forests of teak and bamboo to the epiphytes and strangling figs of the rainforest, extensive plantations of nipa palms and coconut trees, more species of bamboo than any other country except China, and over 1000 varieties of orchid. Thailand exports more orchids than any country in the region. One of the most popular, dendrobium blooms throughout the year, a fitting emblem for a country that warmly welcomes visitors 12 months of the year.

Unfortunately, the rich commercial value of the forests also attracts logging companies.

Sadly, forest depletion is greater in Thailand than any other country in southeast Asia. Still thriving, though, is the areca palm (*Areca catechu*), the fruit of which is mixed with lime and wrapped in the leaf or catkin of the betel vine (*Piper betel*) to make up the semi-addictive 'betel nut' that is consumed as a stimulant. Still common in parts of Thailand, the chewing of betel nuts produces a black stain on the teeth and is regarded as terribly unsophisticated by educated Thais.

Above The lotus flower is sacred to Buddhists, and appreciated by other beings, too, it would appear. Here, a small green frog has found refuge in a lotus bud.

FAUNA

Thailand's incredibly rich and varied fauna is in serious danger as mammals like the Javan and Sumatran rhinoceros and the kouprey become extinct, and forest depletion leads to the wholesale destruction of birds' habitats. The astonishing beauty of the fauna that survives will, one would like to think, spur on efforts to protect and preserve the wildlife.

Just naming some of the bird species that are still easily spotted – the orange-bellied leafbird, the marine oriel, the rusty-naped pitta and snowy-browed flycatcher – gives an idea of the gorgeous colours that light up a walk through the forests of northern Thailand. Khao Yai National Park, a little over 150km (93miles) north of the capital, Bangkok, is the most visited park for some very good reasons. The mountain terrain, tropical forests, effect of two annual monsoons and average temperatures of 23°C (73.5°F) combine to sustain over 20 large mammal species including elephant, tiger, leopard cat, Asiatic black bear, gaur (Indian bison) and serow (a goat antelope).

Perhaps Thailand's best-known mammal is the Siamese cat, also known as the Korat after the name of a large town in northeast Thailand where it was commonly found in the past. Sometime in the late 1950s, Siamese cats were first introduced into the US where they quickly became firm favourites due to their unique silver-blue colour, and the fact that people who are allergic to fur can own this type of cat because it doesn't shed hair when it is stroked. In Thailand, the Siamese is especially associated with good luck.

Left The sly fox butterfly, a member of the nymphalid family, is just one of Thailand's many beautiful insects.

Right Unlike most of the other large cats, tigers enjoy cooling off in rivers and lakes in the heat of the day.

Above The painted stork, similar in looks to the marabou of Africa, can be distinguished by its rather short neck and heavy, straight bill.

Above A boldly striped blister beetle inspects the soft pink petals of a mallow flower.

The Thai People

One in eight Thais lives and works in Bangkok, the capital city, while the dozen or so next largest cities each house an average of just under a quarter of a million citizens.

In a country the size of Texas, with a population of over 60 million people, the bustling urban areas of Thailand account for only a third of the population. That means that most Thais live and work in the countryside.

The typical rural Thai is a rice farmer whose family has worked the land for generations, and whose life cycle is largely determined by the agricultural calendar. The archetypal farming family enjoys a settled existence, with a social and spiritual life that finds expression through the local village community and its colourful cycle of festivals and religious ceremonies.

Compared to this, the urban Thai is viewed by his rural peers as living life at a frenetic and unsettled pace and, especially in the case of Bangkok, this often seems a very reasonable

Above Even features, sparkling eyes, a flawless complexion and a dazzling smile – the Thai are a beautiful people: calm, gentle and mindful of others. Their friendliness, compassion and hospitality is legendary.

Right Rice has been part of Thai culture since as early as 3000BC. Farmers' lives revolve around the demands of their crop and they tend, irrigate and weed for up to 130 days until it matures. Once the harvest is in, it is time to celebrate. As the Thai say 'rice in the barn is like money in the bank'.

interpretation. Bangkok, though, cannot be classed as a typical Thai metropolis. Cities like Chiang Mai and Chiang Rai, both in northern Thailand and each with a population of around 175,000 people, give a much more accurate picture of the pace of Thai life. Here, the rhythm still appears to the average visitor as being enviably placid and sane.

Above The Loi Krathong festival marks the end of the rainy season in November. Small boats, once made of folded leaves but now more commonly of polystyrene, are filled with candles, incense and flowers and floated on lakes and rivers to honour the goddess of water.

Left In simple fishing villages such as this one, the pace of daily life has changed little over the centuries.

Right King Bhumibol, also known as Rama IX, is universally revered and respected. The world's longest reigning monarch, he has ruled since 1946.

THE CULTURAL FABRIC

It is undoubtedly the dynamic vitality of Thai culture that continues to preserve the country's independence of spirit. Nearly every Thai, whatever their religion or ethnic background, speaks the Thai language and this contributes to the strong sense of national identity that most Thais possess.

The sense of nationhood is often expressed through fervent homage to the monarchy. Visitors to the country will witness this in cinemas, where the entire audience will always rise respectfully when the national anthem is played. Even in busy railway stations, the bustling human traffic comes to a momentary pause on a daily basis when loudspeakers broadcast the anthem. Such behaviour is only one aspect of a deep-rooted and honest

Below The belief that things done together are more fulfiling and much more fun than solitary pursuits expresses itself in all sorts of ways, it also lies behind the warm smile that comes so naturally to the Thai people.

regard for decorum that characterizes every nuance of Thai culture. When two Thais meet, they greet each other by bending forward slightly, palms clasped in a prayer-like gesture. People's names are often prefaced by honorific titles that respectfully acknowledge differences in age and status.

Modesty is a guiding principle, one that affects not only the way citizens dress and speak, but also the way they generally comport themselves in the social sphere. Mutual respect, tolerance and understanding are enshrined by a set of unspoken rules that emphasize discretion and moderation.

The most common faux pas committed by Western tourists is to speak or act in a manner that is regarded as uncouth or insulting by the majority of Thais. Speaking loudly or betraying aggression, indeed behaviour of any kind that suggests a confrontational attitude, gains no kudos whatsoever. A Thai often counters such behaviour with a beatific smile and later, in a more private moment, shares mild amusement and bewilderment as the foreigner's antics are described to a colleague.

Above This is a detail of a statue of the Lord Buddha at Sukhothai. Some 95 per cent of Thais are Theravada Buddhists, and Buddhist thought permeates their cultural fabric. It can be summed up in the Thai expression 'do good and receive good; do evil and receive evil'.

Right Resourceful and artistic — many Thai people will display these national attributes even in something as mundane as an attractive arrangement of wares — such as in this stall selling brooms made of palm fronds.

Talk of decorum and proper comportment may create the impression that Thai culture is rather dry and formal, perhaps too tradition-bound for its own good. Fortunately, nothing could be further from the truth, as anyone who has spent time in the country will tell you. What has been left out of the picture so far is the concept of *sanuk*, a Thai word that can loosely but usefully be translated as 'fun'.

Respectful and considerate on one side, Thai culture also acknowledges and celebrates the importance of *sanuk* and in most social situations, whether at work, at home, or relaxing with friends, a liberal dose of *sanuk* will provide essential medicine for the soul.

The spirit of *sanuk* lurks behind the famous Thai smile: an earnest wish to be amiable and avoid confrontation. Visitors who engage with Thais on these terms will enjoy the feeling of having tuned into that spirit – and make some new friends.

Above At the Poi Sang Long festival in Chiang Mai, young boys aged between 7 and 14 are initiated as monks for the duration of the school holidays. They wear ornate costumes and make-up, and are adorned with flowers. It is considered a family honour if a son takes part in this ritual.

Right Unlike monks of western religions, Buddhist monks are encouraged to mingle with their fellow man and are a common sight. The driver of this tuk-tuk will offer the monk transport, his only payment being the honour of doing a service to the faith.

Right Thais display a strong sense of nationality and belonging and take enormous pride in their cultural heritage. The painstaking renovation and restoration of ageing adornments, wall paintings and other ornamental features is the task of skilled craftsmen.

Below These Chinese inspired umbrellas, made in Chiang Mai in northern Thailand, are complex pieces of engineering. They are hand painted with symbols of longevity and good health.

THE HILL TRIBES

It would be hard to find another country in southeast Asia where racial and cultural differences are borne with such genuine acceptance. One of the contributing factors for this is the Thai spirit of tolerance, a facet of a deeply socialized culture that emphasizes togetherness.

Although the hill tribes constitute only about 1 per cent of the total population, their cultural identity is dramatically visible in their forms of traditional dress. Though popular anthropology helps to conjure up the notion of 'primitive' lifestyles, this is inappropriate for the hill tribes of northern Thailand who have managed to retain a place in the cultural landscape of the modern world while protecting their proud heritage and singular identity.

Most populous of the hill tribes are the Karen, whose dress for women indicates their status: white or undyed dresses – sometimes decorated at the seams – for women of marriageable age, and brightly coloured garments for those who are already married.

The Hmong live at high altitudes, above 1000m (3281ft). Their clothes, too, are beautifully embroidered. Skirts and trousers are pleated and decorated with batik designs. The silk jackets are often black, as are their baggy trousers. Ornamental neck rings and heavy jewellery are worn by both sexes on special occasions.

The Lahu also live on high plateaux and their appearance is distinguished by the customary accoutrement of artistically woven shoulder bags, a favourite purchase for visitors in the shops and night markets of Chiang Mai.

The Akha, a small tribe with a population of only around 50,000 originated from Tibet. They also use rich embroidery on their skirts and leggings, but are noted especially for their elaborate head-dresses that use buttons, beads and even coins to colourful effect. The headgear is worn by women on a daily basis.

The Mien number around 42,000 in Thailand, but also live in Myanmar, China, Laos and Vietnam. They too live at high altitudes, settling around mountain springs for their crops of opium, rice and corn. The women wear black, embroidered jackets and pants.

Far left Resplendent in traditional dress, a Hmong woman strides through a field of opium poppies with her toddler on her back. The Hmong grow opium for their own use, along with rice and corn.

Left An Akha tribeswoman puts up her umbrella to protect her elaborate headgear. The Akha are among the poorest of Thailand's hill tribes.

RELIGION

The easy-going demeanour of the Thai people never fails to impress visitors to the country, simply because it comes so effortlessly and seems so natural. In their unwavering display of calm acceptance of the vicissitudes of life, the Thai seem intimately allied to the spirit of Buddhism that pervades this Asian culture.

The lives of some 300,000 monks living in *wats* (monasteries) around the country are engagingly uncloistered and finding a saffron-robed young monk beside you on the seat of a train or bus is a common occurrence. For non-monks, the overcoming of desire and the striving for spiritual merit is very much a matter of everyday behaviour, from laying flowers at a home-made shrine to the cultivation of that quiet spirit that visitors find so disarming. It is difficult to differentiate the reserved deportment that often governs Thai social life from the influence of Buddhism. The religion informs daily life, arising in some degree from its insight that spiritual wellbeing is made manifest through the dignity accorded to daily conduct.

Above It is said that when people hold a stick of incense at prayer their soul becomes transparent and the god can read their thoughts. The smoke acts as a bridge between the world of humanity and that of the spirits. Its fragrance encourages good spirits and carries the wishes of the supplicant to heaven.

Left Buddhist monks at the Jong Klang temple in Mae Hong Son in northern Thailand. Built in the early 19th century by the Thai Yai people, it is Burmese in style. It is here that the Poi Sang Long festival (*see* page 18) is at its most colourful in early March.

Far left Thai Buddhism follows the Theravada school of thought – all things are impermanent, and enlightenment comes from following the Eightfold Path: right understanding, right mindedness, speech, bodily conduct, livelihood, effort, attentiveness and concentration. In this image of the Buddha, he points his right hand at the ground reminding us of the story of his search for enlightenment.

Arts and Crafts

The visitor to Thailand cannot fail to be bowled over by the output and sheer talent of the country's artisans. The range and quality of products, with some crafts associated with particular regions of the country, is material proof of the incredible richness of the cultural landscape. The intricate design used in lacquerware, for instance, is traditionally associated with the Chiang Mai region in the north, partly because this is where the tree flourishes whose sap turns black on exposure to air and creates the sought-after varnish.

While seriously valuable art and craft objects are best admired, in situ, in the palaces and temples of Thailand, enterprising Thais have responded to visitors' wishes to purchase examples of antique Thai art. An organized craft industry has developed, specializing in the reproduction of aesthetically pleasing cultural items. This is not a scam, because the products are not passed off as genuine antiques – but the level of craftsmanship can be very high and prices will reflect this. In Chiang Mai, for example, some shops specialize in reproducing antique Thai and Burmese furniture using old teak wood salvaged from who knows where.

Above One of the delights in the north of Thailand is the opportunity to view and buy embroidered cloth.

Above Incredibly detailed and intricate metalwork reflects a scene from Thailand's rich fabric of myths and legends.

Right In Bangkok's Royal Palace this ornately carved and gilded *garuda*, half bird – half man, supports the spire of the Dusit Maha Prasat, the throne room built for King Rama I.

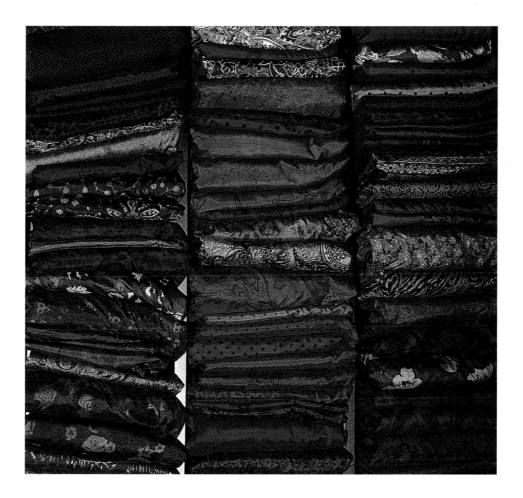

SILK

The northeast of the country, known as Issan, is famous for the quality of its silk. Strangely, the reason for this lies partly in the soil: the land is ideal for mulberry trees, and mulberry leaves are the staple of silkworms that do nothing but eat until they are ready to spin their cocoons out of delicate threads of silk.

Thai silk is generally regarded as superior to that of China and Europe. Not only is it coarser and thicker, it responds to dyeing without losing its soft touch and fine lustre. The most distinctive silk from the northeast is *mudmee*, the threads of which are dyed before being strung on the loom, displaying attractive geometric patterns in the sombre colours that mothers have passed down to their daughters over many generations. Other textiles, especially cotton, provide raw material for craftspeople working all over Thailand and savvy travellers arrive with curtain measurements and sofa sizes jotted down in their notebooks.

Above Bales of woven silk, probably the handiwork of women from the north east of Thailand. These artisans control every stage of the silk-making process from breeding the tiny silkworms to the final dyeing of the cloth.

History

PREHISTORY

Archaeological research confirms that communities were engaged in forms of rice-based agriculture in parts of Thailand by 4000BC, possibly even much earlier, with pottery making an appearance sometime around 3500BC and bronze by 2500BC. The origin of Thailand's first inhabitants remains a hotly debated topic, with different theories pointing to southern China and northern Vietnam.

Above Confusing cave paintings in the 'Viking Cave' in Koh Phi Phi, Krabi province. The cave contains genuine prehistoric stylized human and animal figures, but some 19th-century wag added pictures of Chinese junks just to confuse us all.

Left The ruins of Angkor in northern Cambodia, once capital of the Khmer people. The Khmer empire spread across the region in the first millennium BC. The Khmer ruled northeastern Thailand until the 12th century AD, when the Thai people moved into this area and replaced them relatively peacefully.

EARLY KHMER KINGDOMS

The earliest Thai kingdoms were established in the north of the country, formerly under the rule of the neighbouring Khmer people of present-day Cambodia. Around 1350AD, Ayutthaya, further to the south, became the capital of a new Thai kingdom. Ayutthaya ruled over a large area, including most of Cambodia, and engaged in war with neighbouring Burma whose kings coveted the riches of Siam, as Thailand was called until 1939.

EUROPEAN RELATIONS

The 17th century was a golden age for the Thai kingdom and friendly relations were established with European powers. In 1684, Thai ambassadors presented Louis XIV of France with elephants, rhinoceroses and a letter engraved in gold. In 1767, the old enemy, Burma, destroyed Ayutthaya and it took 10 years before the Thais, under the leadership of General Taskin, expelled the invaders. Taskin's successor, General Chakri, who named himself Rama I and founded a new dynasty, also established a new capital at Bangkok.

The origins of modern Thailand are to be found in the successful attempts of Rama I's successors to retain independence and resist pressure to succumb to Western imperialism.

The kings of neighbouring Burma and Vietnam succumbed, as did the sultans of Malay states to the south. Siam was the only country in Southeast Asia to escape colonial rule. This was in large measure due to the policies of Rama IV and his son Rama V, who ruled between 1851 and 1910. In order to secure Siam's heartland, territory on the periphery was conceded to France, most notably land to the east of the Mekong river.

On the domestic front, a far-reaching programme of modernization got underway and Western advisers were employed to help guide the country's progress. The middle class produced by the process of modernization became restless about absolute royal power and an economic crisis in 1932 helped bring about the transfer of power to a constitutional government, leaving the Chakri dynasty on the throne.

Left A mural from the temple of the Emerald Buddha in Bangkok. The temple was built in the late 18th century by King Rama I, and its murals tell the story of the Ramakien, a mythical tale of celestial beings.

DEMOCRATIC CONSTITUTION

After World War II the country was largely ruled by the army until, in the 1970s, a democratic constitution was introduced. Thailand's democracy, which at times seemed fragile, survived a severe economic crisis in 1997 and, moreover, benefited the following year from a more open constitution being passed into law. The baht, Thailand's currency, has emerged from the 1997 crisis and re-established its stability on the international market.

King Bhumibol (Rama IX) remains on the throne as the world's longest reigning monarch, and his country faces the 21st century with a challenge that would have been familiar to Rama IV and V. Thailand seeks to preserve its independence and its cultural identity while at the same time acknowledging the forces of globalization at work in the world. A fine balancing act is required, but the past kings of Siam managed it successfully and there is good reason to hope and expect that contemporary Thailand and its current monarch will do the same.

Following pages Buddhism is an integral part of Thai life and most boys enter the monkhood at adolescence, thus earning merit for their families and themselves. Not all go on to become monks.

Below The reclining Buddha, a wall painting at Wat Jong Kham in Mae Hong Son, depicts the Buddha at the age of 80 lying down by the bank of a river and passing into Nirvana, the state of non-being.

Bangkok, City of Angels

The light railway system, a reliable riverboat service plying the Chao Praya and a few key bus routes committed to memory make it possible to zip across the city in relative ease and take in the major sites. A visit to the Grand Palace is a must, or join an English-language tour of the National Museum for a fascinating introduction to Thai art, religion and culture. Bangkok is also the shopping capital of Thailand where luggage stores do a brisk trade selling the voluminous suitcases needed to carry surplus purchases home.

Above A bird's-eye view of Bangkok. The loud, fast-paced, throbbing capital city of Thailand presents a bewildering mixture of old and new, venerable past and glittering future.

Right One of many cultural activities in Bangkok is to experience a dance performance – such as is offered at Bangsai Cultural Centre – to marvel at the skill of the dancers and the visual impact of the traditional costumes.

Far right A flaming sunset frames the revered Wat Arun on the bank of the Chao Praya river.

Left The gilded Reclining Buddha in Wat Po temple is 45m (148ft) long and has a beatific smile that stretches some 5m (16ft). Wat Po is a very popular and busy temple and the oldest in Bangkok. Older, indeed, than the capital itself, it was founded in the 17th century and covers an area of 8ha (20 acres).

Below The night skyline of Bangkok, a city where visitors can enjoy the whole range of nightlife, from the techno scene and bars of Patpong to the elaborate, traditional dancing displays of expensive restaurants, or even Thai boxing in one of Bangkok's two national stadiums.

Right The temple of the Emerald Buddha, Grand Palace in Bangkok, has three spires. These depict different architectural styles: a circular *chedi*, a *mondop* with a seven-tiered spire, and a step-spired *prang* – a feature derived from the architecture used in ancient Khmer temples.

Below Beneath the high-tech, futuristic Skyrail that crisscrosses the city, the chaos and bustle of everyday life perseveres.

Below From ancient to ultra modern: Sogo Mall in central Bangkok, where two worlds meet and ancient crafts sit cheerfully beside modern appliances.

Above The Hall of the Buddhas, Wat Po temple in Bangkok. Here, among many other Buddha images, are 394 gilded figures that were created during the reign of Rama I. The statues are in bad repair and depend on the good nature of local people, who will take one away and repair it as part of their dedication to the faith.

Right Since 1782 Chinese people have lived in this part of Bangkok, which has become known as Chinatown. Nowadays it is a bustling shopping and restaurant area.

Left Ornate chedis and a bell tower distinguish Wat Po temple, Thailand's first university. Its walls were once covered in inscriptions and drawings concerning history, literature, farming and medicine. It is still a centre for traditional Thai medicine.

Above The luxurious and expensive Eastern and Oriental Express travels 2034km (1264 miles) between Singapore and Bangkok, stopping briefly at Butterworth, for a guided tour to colonial Georgetown, Penang. Travellers can relax in 1930s style, wining and dining only on the very best, carefully tended in their en-suite cabins by personal stewards.

Right A typical display of seafood available in one of Bangkok's many open-air restaurants. From Royal Thai cuisine to more common cooking, Thai food is one of the most diverse and complex in Asia, offering the visitor an exciting culinary experience.

Above Organized chaos ensues as craft, steered exclusively by women and laden with fresh produce, jostle for position at the Floating Market, Damnoen Saduak, in Ratchaburi province.

Left Outside a Hindu temple, colourful garlands of fresh flowers, as well as coconuts and bunches of bananas are sold to supplicants who wish to make a sacrifice to the gods. Less than half a per cent of the population of Thailand is Hindu.

The Central Plains

Sukhothai was the first capital of a unified Thailand for over a century after 1238. Sukhothai Historical Park sports nearly 200 restored wats, enlivened by lotus ponds and flowering trees. An appealing excursion from here westwards is to the laid-back town of Mae Sot, only 6km (3.7 miles) from Myanmar. A decade ago, this area was rife with smugglers and only intrepid adventurers dared to travel about. Nowadays, a thriving market exists by the safe Thai side of the border.

Above A fisherman navigates home after a hard day's work.

Right In November, the rice harvest gets underway in the rural area west of Nakhon Sawan on the Central Plain.

Left A typical 13th-century figure of the standing Buddha at Sukhothai. The upright position represents the Buddha's descent from heaven in order to help mankind.

Above Shining like living jewels, many colourful dragonflies and damselflies dart along the riverbanks in Thailand's central region.

Above Though Asian elephants can be seen in the wild in some wildlife reserves and national parks, encounters are more likely in logging camps and at tourist venues.

Above Erawan sports many picturesque waterfalls, notably near the park's head-quarters, making it one of Thailand's most popular national parks.

Right A seated Buddha serenely contemplates the pink lotus blossoms on a pond at the ruined city of Sukhothai.

44

Above Bang Pa-In was the summer residence of the 17th-century kings of Siam. This temple stands on an island in the middle of the river, the palace behind it.

Below The pillars supporting an arch of the famous bridge over the river Kwae, frame the floating restaurant on the calm waters below.

Left A partially restored wat among the ruins found at the ancient city of Sukhothai provides a restful spot for devotees and tourists alike.

Above A row of gilded, seated Buddhas at Ayuthaya, once the capital of the Thai kingdom. Many of the ancient temples have been restored and some are still in everyday use.

Right The Bridge of the River Kwae, in Kanchanaburi province, is a popular tourist attraction that can be reached via train ride from Bangkok.

Left The Chinnarat, or Victorious King, at Phitsanulok, is one of Thailand's most revered Buddha images.

Below Left One of the many orchids of Thailand, this Dendrobium Nobile extends its delicate floral sprigs from the lichen-covered trunk of the host tree.

Below Fishing in rivers, streams and on the open ocean is still a mainstay of many Thais and supports numerous families and communities.

The Northern Region

The most popular route from Bangkok is the one heading north to the Chiang Mai region, a 12-hour journey by train or short hop by plane if travelling direct. Moated Chiang Mai can match Bangkok for fine hotels, cuisine and shopping opportunities – but has also managed to retain its quaintness. Route 118 connects Chiang Mai with the far north, the famed Golden Triangle region with Myanmar and Laos on the other side of the Mekong. A perfect area for exploring in a hired vehicle.

Above An attractive stack of umbrellas awaits customers. Thai sun umbrellas, made from bamboo and handpainted in vivid designs and colours, are popular tourist merchandise. Fully collapsible, they are easily transported.

Left Devout Buddhists often adorn parts of revered images, such as these at Wat Phrathat Doi Suthep in Chiang Mai, with thin sheets of gold leaf that are sold in temple complexes.

Right Chedi of Wat Phrathat Doi Suthep, Golden Temple, in Chiang Mai.

Left A detail of the ceramic tile panorama in the Queen's stupa at Doi Inthanon, Chiang Mai.

Left This dancer of Chiang Mai strikes a typical traditional pose. The finger movements and positions are exceptionally expressive; each has a particular meaning.

Far left The Baw Sang factory at Chiang Mai manufactures attractive umbrellas decorated with traditional designs.

Above Colourful parades wend their way through the streets of Chiang Mai for the Songkran or 'water' festival, in celebration of the Thai New Year.

Above This ornate roof detail of Wat Ming Meuang in Chiang Rai, depicts an elephant-like garuda and is typical of Thai architecture.

Right A mosaic-and-glass tiled effigy of Naga, the snake deity, guards the entrance to Wat Phrathat Doi Suthep in Chiang Mai.

Left Imperial in white and gold, the chedi of Wat Jong Klang in Mae Hong Son in the north of Thailand is an impressive sight.

53

Above Detail of the elaborate designs that decorate the temple wall at Wat Phrathat Doi Suthep in Chiang Mai.

Above Alert and ready to strike, this changeable hawk eagle is on the lookout for prey moving about on the forest floor below.

Above In the Hmong villages in northern Thailand, rice is grown, harvested and ground in the time-honoured traditional way.

Right A chedi constructed entirely of flowers forms a colourful backdrop to the meditative serenity of this Buddha statue at the Tha Phae temple in Chiang Mai.

Northeastern Thailand

Thailand's northeast receives less than two per cent of the country's annual quota of visitors, reason enough to head off into this attractive region to experience the local culture, splendid Angkor ruins at Phimai, quality silk at unbeatable prices, and the enticing vista of Laos across the Mekong. Nong Khai, the terminal town, is reached by overnight train from Bangkok. It is situated right by the Mekong and the Friendship Bridge, from where evening boat rides glide travellers down the Thai side of the river.

Above Thai silk is woven in traditional geometric patterns and colours, creating beautiful lengths of fabric.

Right Prasat Hin Phimai is one of the Khmer monuments that have been restored in recent years. Erected during the 12th century, these impressive temple complexes centred on Angkor in present-day Cambodia.

Left The Friendship Bridge that spans the Mekong River, links northern Thailand and Laos.

Above In villages of northeastern Thailand, women can be seen weaving delicate silk cloth at their looms. The cloth is exceptionally fine and well priced.

Below For a reasonable fee visitors can cross the Friendship Bridge that spans the Mekong between Laos and Thailand, and be issued with a visa for Laos.

Right Richly carved stone lintels, such as this one at Muang Tam depicting Uma and Shiva riding on Nandin, are one of the exciting features of the ancient Khmer ruins in northeastern Thailand.

Previous pages Wat Khaek, near Nong Khai, is a venue that contains a vast collection of impressive Hindu and Buddhist sculptures.

Top The fresh catch of the day awaits customers at the fish market in Nakhon Pathom.

Above Spider-like rambutans are among the many exotic fruits that visitors will find at local markets. The name of the strange looking fruit comes from the Malay word for hair, *rambut*.

Left This stone head, originating from a Mon capital of the Dvaravati period (6th–11th century) was found at Nakhon Phatom.

62

Right This close-up view across one of four sacred ponds towards the entrance of Prasat Hin Khao Phanom Rung, a temple complex of the ancient Khmer, is only possible after a steep climb up a monumental, five-tiered staircase.

Below The picturesque course of the Mun river, from Ubon Ratchathani to its junction with the Mekong, is one of the most appealing in the northeastern part of the country. This riverside resort with its floating guest huts is a popular excursion in the region.

The Gulf and Southern Coasts

Eastern Thailand stretches for over 400 km (250 miles) from the capital to the Cambodian border. Idyllic Koh Samet is a favourite with Bangkokians during holiday periods, while larger Koh Chang is a relatively quiet island retreat. Koh Samui offers Chaweng beach, staggeringly beautiful despite the tourist developments, and Cheong Mon, which attracts fewer revellers. Phetchaburi sports Wat Khao Wang, built on the peak of a holy mountain – just one more small part of the surprising magic that is Thailand.

Above Not only are painted fans an attractive and affordable buy, they also provide relief from the oppressive heat and humidity that is experienced in many parts of Thailand.

Left Some 50 limestone islands make up Ang Thong archipelago – declared a national marine park in 1980. They can be reached by boat from Koh Samui.

Right Fishermen return home at the end of the day.

Above Shadow puppets are skilfully crafted. They have moving joints and are elaborately decorated. Most puppet productions centre on legendary episodes of deities and their demonic adversaries.

Right The gilded images of the Buddha at Wat Mahathat in Phetchaburi, a town whose history dates back to the ancient Khmer period.

Above Thatched bungalows offer luxury accommodation for visitors to the idyllic Koh Chan National Park.

Above Left Spirit houses, found near most homes, hotels and businesses in Thailand, are erected to placate the spirits who inhabited the area before humans settled there. They are often adorned with flowers.

Left Salt crystals are harvested in shallow, dry lakes. Old and young alike labour in these salt works. It is back-breaking work for very little remuneration by western standards.

Following pages Paradise on earth: an endless stretch of palm-fringed beach on Koh Samui.

Above The coastal wetlands of Khao Sam Roi Yot Marine National Park harbour a diverse collection of waders, water- and shorebirds, such as the purple heron, spot-billed pelican and purple swamphen.

Right The vividly coloured purple swamphen is just of the many wetland birds that can be seen in the freshwater marshes of Khao Sam Roi Yot.

Left The Big Buddha seems to preside watchfully over the breathtaking tropical paradise visitors discover on Koh Samui.

Left Prows of longtail boats on Phi Phi Island, adorned with the rowers' head dress and flower garlands.

Above Along the east coast you can see *korlae*, fishing boats built and painted by Muslim fishermen. The finest examples come from the boat yards of Saiburi.

Right Mu Koh Surin Marine National Park is a magnet for divers. Colourful coral reefs and their inhabitants, such as this solitary longfin bannerfish and a school of other reef fishes provide a fascinating glimpse of underwater Thailand.

Above Tradition and technology go hand in hand along Thailand's coast, where modern outboard motors power small, traditionally hand-built fishing boats, such as here, on Phi Phi Island.

Right Favourable wind conditions, warm seas and a sunny disposition make the Gulf Coast of Thailand as well as the southern islands a favourite with windsurfers. Many of the upmarket tourist facilities offer hire equipment for those visitors who would like to harness the wind and surf in style.

Far right Beautiful Koh Phi Phi actually consists of two islands, Phi Phi Don and the uninhabited Phi Phi Ley. Phi Phi Don attracts large numbers of visitors; Phi Phi Ley can be visited on daily boat trips.

Right Cruising between the islands, visitors can often spot inquisitive dolphins swimming close to the boat, or darting in front or alongside the speeding craft. The intelligent sea mammals seem undeniably fascinated with their human visitors.

Below Phuket is justifiably famous for its amazing beach, but that is not the only attraction here. Buddhist temples, such as Chalong, as well as mosques and Chinese shrines wait to be explored.

Right Ornately decorated demons and temple guards are seen all around Thailand, as well as here at Wat Bang Riang in Phang-Nga.

Below Right Traditional Thai music employs many different instruments. Note the bamboo xylophones in the background.

Below World destinations are marked at this lookout point in Phuket, so international visitors can turn in the direction of their country and send silent greetings home if they wish.

Above On Khao Lak beach, a forest of handwritten signs advertises everything from manicures to henna painting, as well as Thai- and foot massages.

Below Krabi, arguably the most beautiful province of the south, has a wonderful coastline whose karst formations attract climbers and cavers.

Left An early morning view of rafthouses perched on a lake in Khao Sok National Park, Southern Thailand. The quaint wooden houses are run as a hotel by the park's headquarters.

PHOTOGRAPHIC ACKNOWLEDGEMENTS

Copyright rests with the following photographers and/or their agents. Key to Locations: t = top; tl = top left; tr = top right; b = bottom; bl = bottom left; br = bottom right; l = left; r = right; c = centre; cl = centre left; cr = centre right. (No abbreviation is given for pages with a single image, or pages on which all photographs are by same photographer.)

AA AA World Travel Library; **AAP** Artasia Press (**WK** Wachara Kireewong); **AI** Asia Images (**JE** John Everingham); **AB** Anders Blomqvist; **AE** Alain Evrard; **APA** Axiom Photographic Agency (**MO** Mikihiko Ohta); **CO** Christine Osborne; **DB** David Bowden; **EN** Eric Nathan; **FF** Ffotograff (**MA** Mary Andrews, **MG** Mike Greenslade, **JJ** Jill Jones, **JR** Jill Ranford, **NT** Nick Tapsell); **GC** Gerald Cubitt; **GP** Globe Press (**JH** J Houyvet); **GZC** Geraldine Z Cupido; **JB** John Borthwick; **JJ** Jack Jackson; **JS** Jeroen Snijders; **KM** Kelvin Marshall; **MV** Mireille Vautier; **OI** Oceanic Impression; **PD** Paul Dymond; **SCPL** Sylvia Cordaiy Photo Library (**RNB** R Norman Barret, **CH** C Holmberg, **KS** Kjell Sandved, **JS** Johnathan Smith); **TI** Travel Ink (**CB** Charcrit Boonsom, **ME** Martyn Evans, **PF** Patrick Ford, **AH** Allan Hartley, **PK** Peter Kingsford, **PT** Pauline Thornton).

Page	Loc	Photo		Page	Loc	Photo		Page	Loc	Photo		Page	Loc	Photo
cover		AB		18	b	TI/PT		40		FF/JJ		59		AB
back cover		AE		19	t	DB		41		GC		60/61		MV
1		AI		19	b	AE		42	tl	GC		62	t	FF/JR
2		AE		20		GP			tr	GC			bl	FF/JJ
3		AE		21		AE			b	AAP/WK			br	CO
4		AI/JE		22		JS		43		APA/MO		63	t	AI/JE
5	t	GP		23	l	AE		44		APA/MO			b	GC
	bl	AI/JE			tr	FF/MG		45	t	AI/JE		64	t	TI/AH
	br	AAP/WK		24	t	AA			b	CO			b	AI/JE
6	t	KM			bl	JS		46	t	TI/CB		65		FF/MA
	b	AE			br	PD			b	GC		66	t	FF/JJ
7		SCPL/JS		25		AA		47	tl	JS			b	AA
8		AB		26		AB			bl	GC		67	tl	KM
9	l	OI		27		AB			br	JS			tr	TI/ME
	tr	AE		28		AE		48	t	GZC			b	CO
	br	OI		29		AE			b	JS		68/69		AAP/WK
10	t	AB		30/31		AE		49		AE		70		EN
	b	JB		32	t	JB		50		AE		71		GC
11	t	DB			b	JB		51	t	AA		72		SCPL/JS
	b	AI/JE		33		AE			b	JS		73	t	AA
12		SCPL/KS		34	t	TI/PF		52		TI/CB			b	OI
13	tl/tr	GC			b	SCPL/JS		53	t	AE		74	t	JS
	b	AA		35	t	AE			cl	AA			b	GP/JH
14	t	AE			bl	JS			br	TI/PK		75		AI/JE
	b	CO			br	JS		54	tl/b	AE		76	t	JJ
15	t	FF/JJ		36		TI/AH		54	tr	GC			b	JB
	b	SCPL/JS		37	t	AB		55		AE		77	bl	AB
16	t	AA			b	AA		56		GC			tr	JB
	b	AE		38	t	JB		57	t	SCPL/CH			br	JB
17	t	JS			b	JS			b	AI/JE		78		AAP/WK
	b	SCPL/RNB		39	t	AA		58	t	FF/NT		79	t	AA
18	t	AE			b	FF/JJ			b	AI/JE			b	AI/JE

First published in 2003 by
New Holland Publishers Ltd
London • Cape Town
Sydney • Auckland
www.newhollandpublishers.com

86 Edgware Road, London, W2 2EA
United Kingdom

80 McKenzie Street, Cape Town, 8001
South Africa

14 Aquatic Drive, Frenchs Forest, NSW 2086
Australia

218 Lake Road, Northcote, Auckland
New Zealand

Copyright © 2003 New Holland Publishers (UK) Ltd
Copyright © 2003 in text: Sean Sheehan
Copyright © 2003 in photographs: Individual
photographers and/or their agents as listed above.

All rights reserved. No part of this publication may be reproduced, stored in a retrieval system or transmitted, in any form or by any means, electronic, mechanical, photocopying, recording or otherwise, without the prior written permission of the publishers and copyright holders.

ISBN 1 84330 454 6

Publishing managers Claudia Dos Santos, Simon Pooley
Designer Sheryl Buckley
Picture researcher Karla Kik
Production Myrna Collins
Cartographer Marisa Galloway
Proofreader Katja Splettstoesser

Reproduction by Hirt & Carter (Cape) Pty Ltd
Printed and bound in Malaysia by
Times Offset (M) Sdn. Bhd.

10 9 8 7 6 5 4 3 2 1

NEW HOLLAND

80